Off Like the Wind!

The First Ride
of the
Pony Express

Michael P. Spradlin

Paintings by **Layne Johnson**

Walker & Company
New York

"The pony-rider was usually a little bit of a man, brim full of spirit and endurance.
No matter what time of the day or night his watch came on, and no matter whether
it was winter or summer, raining, snowing, hailing, or sleeting . . . he must
be always ready to leap into the saddle and be off like the wind!"
—Mark Twain, *Roughing It*

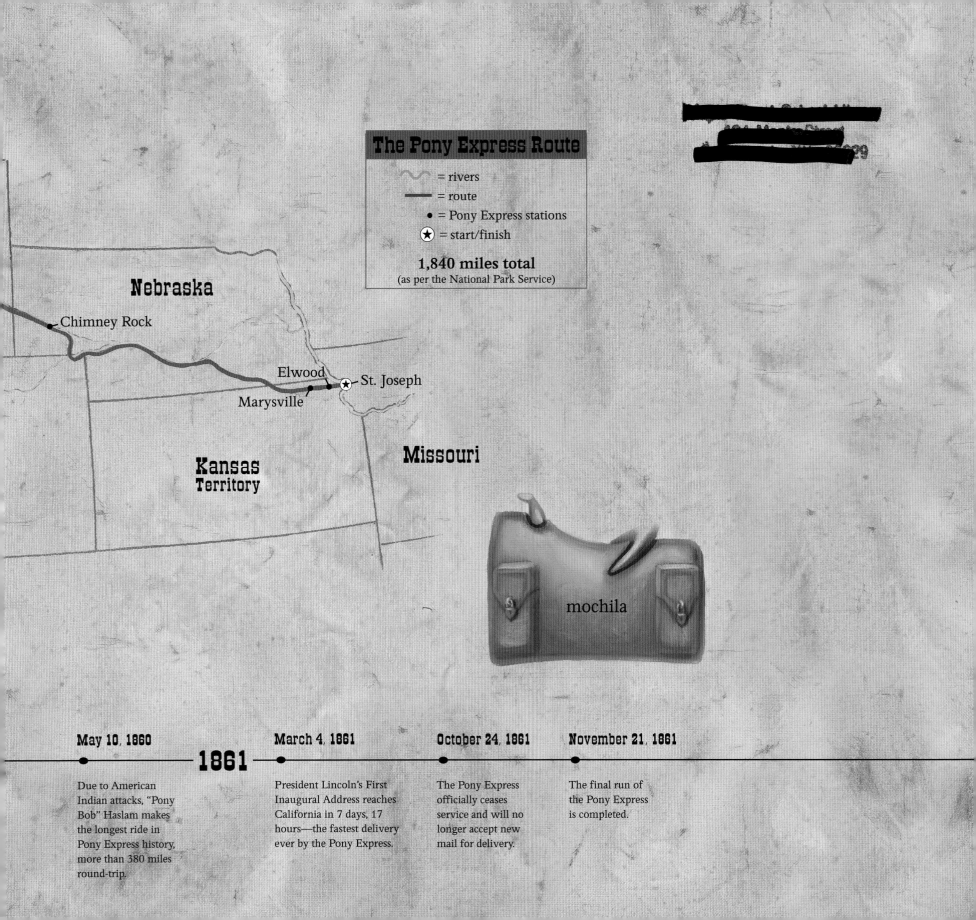

The Pony Express Route

∿ = rivers

━━ = route

• = Pony Express stations

(★) = start/finish

1,840 miles total
(as per the National Park Service)

Nebraska

Chimney Rock

Elwood
Marysville
St. Joseph

Kansas
Territory

Missouri

mochila

May 10, 1860

Due to American Indian attacks, "Pony Bob" Haslam makes the longest ride in Pony Express history, more than 380 miles round-trip.

1861

March 4, 1861

President Lincoln's First Inaugural Address reaches California in 7 days, 17 hours—the fastest delivery ever by the Pony Express.

October 24, 1861

The Pony Express officially ceases service and will no longer accept new mail for delivery.

November 21, 1861

The final run of the Pony Express is completed.

To my aunt Miney, Mrs. Elmina Hackworth,
my all-time favorite aunt
—M. P. S.

To my first art teacher, Clara Skinner—
thanks for instilling in me a love of painting
—L. J.

First published in the United States of America in March 2010 by
Walker Publishing Company, Inc.
A division of Bloomsbury Publishing, Inc.
Visit Walker & Company's Web site at www.bloomsburykids.com

For information about permission to reproduce selections from this book, write to
Permissions, Walker & Company, 175 Fifth Avenue, New York, New York 10010

Library of Congress Cataloging-in-Publication Data
Spradlin, Michael P.
Off like the wind! : the first ride of the pony express / by Michael P. Spradlin ; illustrated by Layne Johnson.
p.   cm.
ISBN: 978-0-8027-9652-3 (hardcover) • ISBN: 978-0-8027-9653-0 (reinforced)
1. Pony express—History—Juvenile literature. 2. Postal service—United States—History—Juvenile literature.
3. West (U.S.)—History—1860–1890—Juvenile literature. I. Johnson, Layne, ill. II. Title.
HE6375.P65S77 2010   383'.1430978—dc22   2009010827

Book design by Danielle Delaney
Typeset in Perrywood MT Std
Art created with oils on canvas

Printed in China by Printplus Limited, Shenzhen, Guangdong
2 4 6 8 10 9 7 5 3 (hardcover)
2 4 6 8 10 9 7 5 3 (reinforced)

In the early days of the American frontier, settlers in the state of California and in the western territories were eager to receive mail from their families back east. It took a great amount of time and expense for letters to travel from the east coast all the way west. Most deliveries came by ship and often took months to arrive.

Three businessmen—William H. Russell, Alexander Majors, and William B. Waddell—had made their fortune hauling goods by wagon across the prairies and deserts of the West. They believed they could deliver mail along the Central Route that crossed the western states, through the South Pass of the Rocky Mountains, on to California.

Their idea was to build a series of stations every ten to fifteen miles along this route and carry mail on horseback, with riders changing horses at each station. If successful, they hoped the U.S. government would grant them a contract. They bought horses and hired riders, and in less than six months they were ready to begin.

This new venture would be a division of their Central Overland California and Pike's Peak Express Company. It became known as the Pony Express.

DAY 1

7:30 p.m.
April 3, 1860
St. Joseph, Missouri

In the streets of St. Joseph, Missouri, a large crowd waits for the train to arrive. This train, nicknamed "The Hannibal," holds the mail the first Pony Express rider will carry west.

A rider named Johnny Fry will be the first man to take this historic ride—one that will last about eleven days in total. Fry will ride the first leg of the mail delivery, a distance of about eighty miles. He will change horses every ten to fifteen miles at relay stations. There are about 160 stations placed along the nearly 2,000-mile trail.

The Pony Express will carry the mail from St. Joseph, Missouri, to Sacramento, California, in small locked pouches called *mochilas*. The first mochila will carry eighty-five pieces of mail, including a special edition of the *St. Joseph Daily Gazette* printed on lightweight paper. To send a letter by Pony Express costs five dollars per half ounce, an enormous sum of money at the time.

Finally the train arrives and the mail is transferred to the mochila. Johnny Fry climbs into the saddle. The mayor of St. Joseph, Jeff Thompson, makes a brief speech to the assembled crowd: "Citizens of St. Joseph, I bid you give three cheers for the Pony Express—three cheers for the first overland passage of the United States mail. Hip, hip, hurrah! Hip, hip, hurrah! Hip, hip, hurrah!" The mayor smacks Fry's horse, Sylph, on the rump, and the Pony Express begins its ride into history.

Once Johnny Fry and Sylph cross the Missouri River on a ferryboat, Fry must then guide the horse through the thick woods to Elwood Station—the first swing station, or temporary stopover—on the trail. In less than two minutes, Fry changes horses and is on his way to the next station. When he arrives at the first home station—or more fully equipped stopover—in Marysville, Kansas, Fry hands off the mochila to a relief rider. Fry's part of the ride is done until the eastbound mochila arrives from California.

Riders spend their downtime at the home station doing chores to help the station master keep things running smoothly. They never know how long they will have to wait for the next mochila to arrive, but it is usually at least a few days.

Day 2
April 4, 1860
Kansas Territory

Just before sunrise, the next rider crosses the wide prairie, where the tall grasses are home to several large herds of buffalo. As he crests a ridge, a giant herd of buffalo blocks his path. He carefully steers his horse through the herd so as not to spook the skittish animals. But a rainstorm is approaching. . . .

Thunder cracks and lightning strikes the ground nearby, and the nervous buffalo stampede!

Forced to gallop along with the rampaging herd, the rider and his horse are knocked about by the tidal wave of animals. Many times the rider nearly loses his grip on the horse, but he holds on desperately, terrified of being trampled. Finally the buffalo stop running and the rider is able to work his way back to the trail.

DAY 3

April 5, 1860
Chimney Rock Station
Nebraska Territory

Chimney Rock is a famous landmark for pioneers traveling westward and can be seen from miles away. The conditions at Chimney Rock Station are very primitive. Most of the buildings are in poor repair, and even tents are used for shelter. The rider is fed a simple meal of bacon, beans, and corn bread. Life at Chimney Rock, and at many of the stations along the trail, can be hazardous, for nearby native tribes will frequently raid the station to steal horses and supplies.

Pony Express riders carry at least one Colt pistol, but they are under orders not to fight back against attackers unless they have no choice. The four hundred Pony Express horses were chosen for their great speed and endurance, so riders are told to outrun any threats. Near Chimney Rock Station, a small band of American Indians chases the rider for several miles. As arrows fly all around him, he bends low and spurs the horse to a fast gallop—escaping danger and reaching the next station safely.

Day 4

April 6, 1860
Devil's Gate Station
Wyoming Territory

By Day 4, the mail has traveled more than eight hundred miles from its beginning at St. Joseph. The rider now reaches Devil's Gate, a large rock gorge that is hundreds of feet deep and has been carved by the Sweetwater River for thousands of years. Here the air is dry and hot, but luckily the trail follows rivers and streams, so there is plenty of water for the horse and rider.

While on the trail, the rider must keep a constant watch for danger of all kinds. As he approaches the station, he surprises a pack of wolves feeding on a buffalo. His horse is startled by the wolves and dashes away. The wolves chase after them and the rider struggles to control the horse until the wolves give up. A spooked horse is one of the most dangerous parts of a Pony Express rider's job. Riders could be seriously injured or even killed if thrown from a horse.

Day 5
April 7, 1860
Pacific Springs Station
Wyoming Territory

The rider now follows a route crossing wide sagebrush-covered plains, and finally he reaches the Continental Divide. He crosses through South Pass, which is the easiest route through the Rockies. At Pacific Springs Station, the mail has nearly reached the halfway point on the trail and is now about five and a half days from Sacramento.

DAY 6

April 8, 1860
Jordan River
Utah Territory

On the sixth day, the rider crosses into Utah Territory.
Because this part of the route is dry and arid, many of
the stations along the trail must have water brought in
by wagon for the horses and riders.

This is also a very dangerous part of the trail as it
crosses through territory that belongs to the Pah Ute
tribe. The Pah Ute people are angry with American
miners for breaking treaties and taking away their
lands, and Pony Express riders must be constantly on
the watch for an attack.

DAY 7

April 9, 1860
Sportsman's Hall Station
Nevada Territory

At Sportsman's Hall, another home station along the trail, Warren Upson waits for the arrival of the first eastbound mochila from rider Billy Hamilton. Hamilton had left Sacramento on April 3, and he will return there with the westbound mochila. He is an experienced horseman and will need every bit of his skill to make it through the part of the trail that includes the high mountains of the Sierra Nevada range. When he arrives at Sportsman's Hall, he is relieved of the eastbound mochila by Warren Upson.

Even in the springtime, the snow in the mountains is still deep. Because blizzards happen frequently—and sometimes without warning—it is easy to become lost in the blinding snow, which can drift more than twenty feet high. A few miles out of Sportsman's Hall, a snowstorm whips up and Upson is forced to dismount, leading his horse through the cold and the swirling snow on foot. It takes him nearly a full day to arrive at the next station, which can usually be reached in a few hours on horseback.

DAY 8

April 10, 1860
Mormon Tavern Station
California

While Billy makes his way back toward California, the citizens there are eager for the Pony Express to arrive. For weeks local newspapers have been urging citizens to support "the Pony" despite the high cost of using the service.

Over the next eighteen months, communication with the eastern states will become critical as the nation moves closer to civil war. In fact, in the spring of 1861, Pony Express riders will carry copies of President Abraham Lincoln's Inaugural Address from Missouri to California in only seven days, seventeen hours.

DAY 9

2 p.m.
April 11, 1860
Placerville Station
California

Billy keeps the mail moving, and as he begins to reach the small towns and settlements of California, he is cheered by settlers who have waited eagerly for a glimpse of the famous "Pony."

Many settlers and miners in the West had not had news or letters from their families for months or sometimes years. They are overjoyed to know that the news and information can now arrive so quickly.

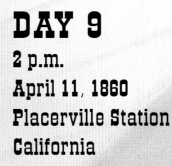

DAY 10

April 12, 1860
California–Nevada Border

While Billy Hamilton rides on toward Sacramento, back at Marysville, Kansas, the eastbound mochila has arrived at the station. In the very early days of the service, some Pony riders carry a bugle or horn to blow, alerting the station that they are coming. Hearing the signal, the station masters can have the next horse saddled and ready to go. Eventually riders will give up the horns to save weight.

When the rider from the west skids to a stop at Marysville, the mochila is transferred to Johnny Fry's horse. Fry leaps into the saddle and rides hard toward St. Joseph.

DAY 11

April 13, 1860

Western Terminus of the Pony Express

Sacramento, California

On April 13, 1860, Billy Hamilton reaches Sacramento with the first westbound mail delivered by Pony Express. Hamilton is surprised to find people cheering him on as he rides through the city. He delivers the mail to the Alta Telegraph office—from there, the mail is taken by steamship to San Francisco.

DAY 11

April 13, 1860
St. Joseph, Missouri

Back in St. Joseph, Johnny Fry rides into town with the first eastbound mail from California. Bands play, cannons fire, and people cheer throughout the city. From there, the mail is put on a train headed east.

Many people had refused to believe that the Pony Express could ever deliver the mail. But in ten and a half days' time, mail from the East and the West has crossed more than half a continent. Three cheers for the Pony Express!

AUTHOR'S NOTE

The Pony Express is an example of American "can-do" spirit at its finest. However, separating the truth from the legend has been a daunting task for historians. Following the service's suspension, most—if not all—of the official records were lost (or more likely destroyed, to avoid their use in lawsuits). Many payroll and employment records were never recovered, making it difficult to accurately identify riders and even exact locations of stations along the trail.

We do know Johnny Fry left St. Joseph, Missouri, on April 3, 1860, with the first westbound mochila. His counterpart, Billy Hamilton, left Sacramento, California, on April 3, with the eastbound mochila, handing off to Warren Upson. Beyond those three men, especially in the first days of the service, remaining riders in the middle of the route cannot be verified with a reasonable degree of certainty. Because of this, the days in between Fry, Hamilton, and Upson's journeys are handled in this book as a composite of the rides taken by many riders throughout the Pony Express's history. At each stage, documented information about the terrain and the obstacles faced there was combined with established accounts of the interactions with native tribes and wildlife such as buffalo and wolves. We know with certainty that these events transpired; what can never be known is exactly when and where.

In terms of the overall impact on the native tribes and wildlife of the American West, the Pony Express left a relatively small footprint. Most native tribes allowed riders to pass through their lands without incident. On May 7, 1860, the Pah Ute uprising began when several warriors raided Williams Station in Nevada. The Pah Utes were angry at years of abuse by white miners and chose the station as a target of convenience. This is the only documented instance of major conflict.

On October 24, 1861, about eighteen months after the first Pony Express riders left St. Joseph and Sacramento, the transcontinental telegraph line was completed. Messages and news could now be sent across the country in minutes, and the Pony Express was no longer needed.

Despite the inconsistencies in its history, the determination and courage of the men who rode the two thousand–mile Pony Express trail, bringing the nation closer together at a critical period in our history, can never be denied. Hurrah for the Pony Express!

Suggestions for Further Reading

Benson, Joe. *The Traveler's Guide to the Pony Express Trail.* Helena, MT: Falcon, 1995.

Coleman, Wim, and Pat Perrin. *The Transcontinental Railroad and the Great Race to Connect the Nation: The Wild History of the American West.* Berkeley Heights, NJ: Myreportlinks, 2006.

King, David. *Children's Encyclopedia of American History.* New York, NY: Dorling Kindersley, 2003.

Moeller, Bill, and Jan Moeller. *The Pony Express: A Photographic History.* Missoula, MT: Mountain Press Publishing Company, 2003.

Bibliography

Billington, R. A. *Westward Expansion: A History of the American Frontier, Abridged 6th ed.* Albuquerque: University of New Mexico Press, 2001.

Burton, Richard Francis. *The Look of the West, 1860: Across the Plains to California.* Lincoln, NE: University of Nebraska Press, 1963.

Corbett, Christopher. *Orphans Preferred: The Twisted Truth and Lasting Legend of the Pony Express.* New York, NY: Random House, 2003.

Sell, Henry Blackman, and Victor Weybright. *Buffalo Bill and the Wild West.* New York, NY: Oxford University Press, 1955.

Twain, Mark. *Roughing It.* Edited by Harriet E. Smith and Edgar M. Branch. Berkeley, CA: University of California Press, 2002.

Visscher, William Lightfoot. *A Thrilling and Truthful History of the Pony Express: Or, Blazing the Westward Way, and Other Sketches and Incidents of Those Stirring Times.* Chicago, IL: Charles T. Powner Co., 1946.

Pony Express Web Sites for Young Readers

www.pocanticohills.org/ponyexpress/ponyexpress.htm

www.42explore2.com/pony.htm

www.americanwest.com/trails/pages/ponyexp1.htm

For More Information on the History of the Pony Express

The National Pony Express Association   www.xphomestation.com

The Pony Express National Museum, St. Joseph, Missouri   www.ponyexpress.org

The Pony Express National Historic Trail, National Park Service   www.nps.gov/poex

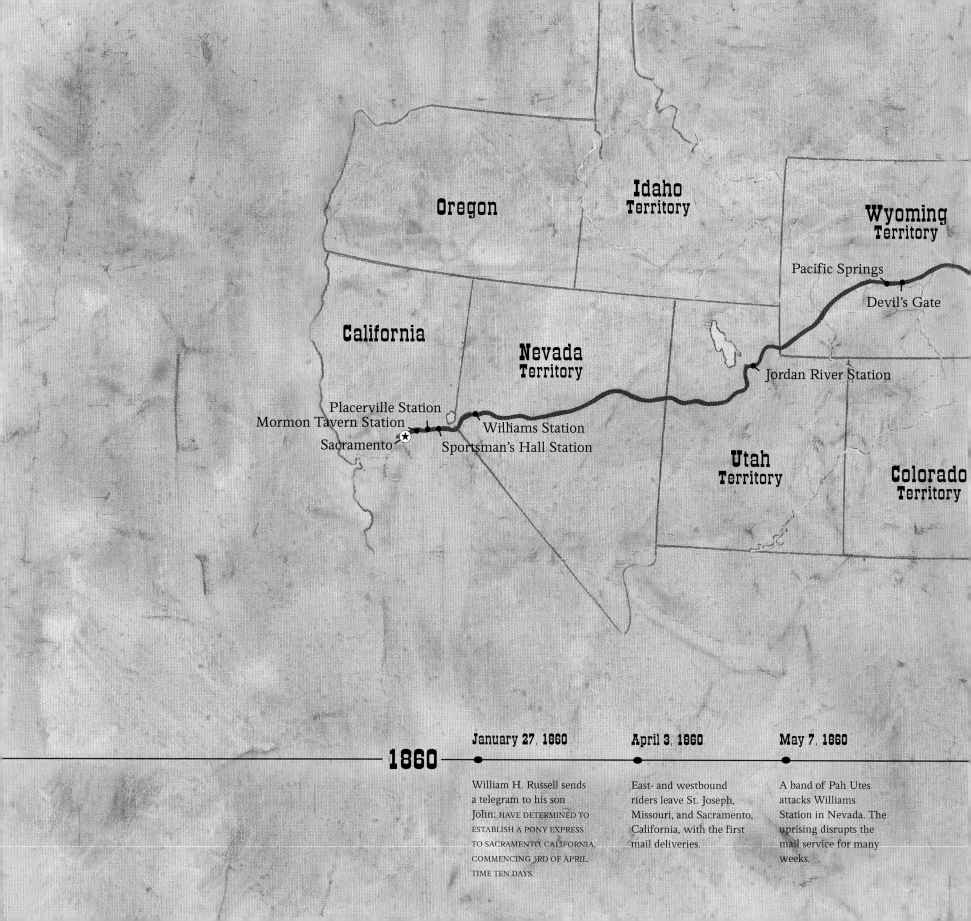

Oregon

Idaho
Territory

Wyoming
Territory

Pacific Springs

Devil's Gate

California

Nevada
Territory

Jordan River Station

Placerville Station
Mormon Tavern Station
Sacramento
Williams Station
Sportsman's Hall Station

Utah
Territory

Colorado
Territory

1860

January 27, 1860

William H. Russell sends
a telegram to his son
John: HAVE DETERMINED TO
ESTABLISH A PONY EXPRESS
TO SACRAMENTO, CALIFORNIA,
COMMENCING 3RD OF APRIL.
TIME TEN DAYS.

April 3, 1860

East- and westbound
riders leave St. Joseph,
Missouri, and Sacramento,
California, with the first
mail deliveries.

May 7, 1860

A band of Pah Utes
attacks Williams
Station in Nevada. The
uprising disrupts the
mail service for many
weeks.